Crocheted Snugglers

Easy Blankets for Baby

Martingale
Create with Confidence

Crocheted Snugglers: Easy Blankets for Baby

© 2013 by Martingale®

Martingale

19021 120th Ave. NE, Ste. 102

Bothell, WA 98011-9511 USA

ShopMartingale.com

Printed in China

18 17 16 15 14 13   8 7 6 5 4 3 2 1

Library of Congress Cataloging-in-Publication Data is available upon request.

ISBN: 978-1-60468-317-2

Mission Statement

Dedicated to providing quality products and service to inspire creativity.

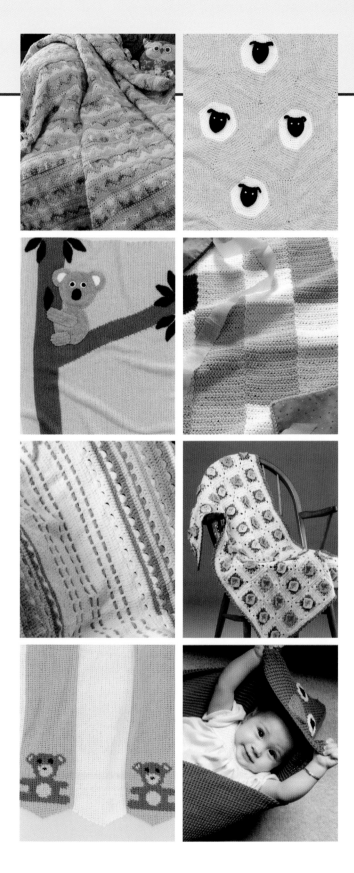

Contents

Krazy Kids

What fun your kids will have cuddling in this cheerful blanket!

Skill Level
◼◼◼◻ Intermediate

Size
44" x 50", excluding edging

Materials
Yarn: All yarns are 100% acrylic worsted-weight yarn (4)
  A: 975 yds (multicolor)
  B: 512 yds (pink)
  C: 778 yds (yellow)
  D: 512 yds (lime)
Hook: Size H-8 (5 mm) crochet hook or size to obtain gauge
Notions: Tapestry needle

Gauge
14 sc and 14 rows = 4"

Blanket
To change color, work until 2 lps of last st remain on hook. With new color, YO and draw through 2 lps on hook. Cut old color.

With A, ch 152.

Row 1 (RS): Sc in 2nd ch from hook and in each rem ch. Turn—151 sc.

Row 2: Ch 1, sc in first sc, *hdc in next sc, dc in next sc, work 3 tr in next sc, dc in next sc, hdc in next sc, sc in next sc; rep from * across, changing to B in last sc. Turn—201 sts.

Row 3: With B, ch 1, sc2tog over first 2 sts, *sc in next 2 sts, work 3 sc in next st, sc in next 2 sts, sc3tog over next 3 sts; rep from * another 23 times, sc in next 2 sts, work 3 sc in next st, sc in next 2 sts, sc2tog over next 2 sts. Turn.

Row 4: Rep row 3, changing to C in last st. Turn.

Row 5: With C, ch 3, tr in next st (counts as a tr dec on this and following rows), *dc in next sc, hdc in next sc, sc in next sc, hdc in next sc, dc in next sc, tr3tog over next 3 sc; rep from * another 23 times, dc in next sc, hdc in next sc, sc in next sc, hdc in next sc, dc in next sc, tr2tog over next 2 sc. Turn—151 sts.

Row 6: Ch 1, sc in each st, changing to D in last st. Turn.

Row 7: With D, ch 1, sc in each sc. Turn.

Row 8: Ch 1, sc in first sc, *hdc in next sc, dc in next sc, work 3 tr in next sc, dc in next sc, hdc in next sc, sc in next sc; rep from * across, changing to A in last sc—201 sts. Turn.

Row 9: With A, ch 1, sc2tog over first 2 sts, *sc in next 2 sts, work 3 sc in next st, sc in next 2 sts, sc3tog over next 3 sts; rep from * another 23 times, sc in next 2 sts, work 3 sc in next st, sc in next 2 sts, sc2tog over next 2 sts. Turn.

Row 10: Rep row 9, changing to B in last st. Turn.

Row 11: With B, ch 3, tr in next sc, *dc in next sc, hdc in next sc, sc in next sc, hdc in next sc, dc in next sc, tr3tog over next 3 sc; rep from * another 23 times, dc in next sc, hdc in next sc, sc in next sc, hdc in next sc, dc in next sc, tr2tog over next 2 sc—151 sts. Turn.

Row 12: Ch 1, sc in each st, changing to C in last st. Turn.

Row 13: With C, ch 1, sc in each sc. Turn.

Row 14: Ch 1, sc in first sc, *hdc in next sc, dc in next sc, work 3 tr in next sc, dc in next sc, hdc in next sc, sc in next sc; rep from * across, changing to D in last sc—201 sts. Turn.

Row 15: With D, sc2tog over first 2 sts, *sc in next 2 sts, work 3 sc in next st, sc in next 2 sts, sc3tog over next 3 sts; rep from * another 23 times, sc in next 2 sts, work 3 sc in next st, sc in next 2 sts, sc2tog over next 2 sts. Turn.

Row 16: Rep row 15, changing to A in last st. Turn.

Row 17: With A, ch 3, tr in next sc, *dc in next sc, hdc in next sc, sc in next sc, hdc in next sc, dc in next sc, tr3tog over next 3 sc; rep from * another 23 times, dc in next sc, hdc in next sc, sc in next sc, hdc in next sc, dc in next sc, tr2tog over next 2 sc. Turn—151 sts.

Row 18: Ch 1, sc in each st, changing to B in last st. Turn.

Row 19: With B, ch 1, sc in each sc. Turn.

Row 20: Ch 1, sc in first sc, *hdc in next sc, dc in next sc, work 3 tr in next sc, dc in next sc, hdc in next sc, sc in next sc; rep from * across, changing to C in last sc. Turn—201 sts.

Row 21: With C, sc2tog over first 2 sts, *sc in next 2 sts, work 3 sc in next st, sc in next 2 sts, sc3tog over next 3 sts; rep from * another 23 times, sc in next 2 sts, work 3 sc in next st, sc in next 2 sts, sc2tog over next 2 sts. Turn.

Row 22: Rep row 21, changing to D in last st.

Row 23: With D, ch 3, tr in next sc, *dc in next sc, hdc in next sc, sc in next sc, hdc in next sc, dc in next sc, tr3tog over next 3 sc; rep from * another 23 times, dc in next sc, hdc in next sc, sc in next sc, hdc in next sc, dc in next sc, tr2tog over next 2 sc. Turn—151 sts.

Row 24: Ch 1, sc in each st, changing to A in last st. Turn.

Row 25: With A, ch 1, sc in each sc. Turn.

Row 26: Ch 1, sc in first sc, *hdc in next sc, dc in next sc, work 3 tr in next sc, dc in next sc, hdc in next sc, sc in next sc; rep from * across, changing to B in last sc. Turn—201 sts.

Rows 27–122: Work rows 3–26 another 4 times.

Rows 123–138: Rep rows 3–18 once more. At end of last row, do not change to B. Turn.

Edging

Rnd 1 (RS): Cont with A, ch 1, work 3 sc in first sc—corner made; sc in next 149 sc, work 3 sc in last sc—corner made; working along next side in ends of rows, sk first row, work 159 sc evenly spaced to last row, sk last row; working along lower edge in unused lps of beg ch, work 3 sc in first lp—corner made; sc in next 149 lps, work 3 sc in last lp—corner made; working along next side in ends of rows, sk first row, work 159 sc evenly spaced to last row, sk last row; join in first sc—628 sc.

Rnd 2: Ch 1, sc in same sc as joining and in next 3 sc, ch 7, sk next 4 sc, work (sc in next 4 sc, ch 7, sk next 4 sc) 18 times, sc in next 4 sc, ch 7, sk next 5 sc, work (sc in next 4 sc, ch 7, sk next 4 sc) 18 times, sc in next 4 sc, ch 7, sk next 5 sc, work (sc in next 4 sc, ch 7, sk next 4 sc) 19 times, sc next 4 sc, ch 7, sk next 5 sc, work (sc in next 4 sc, ch 7, sk next 4 sc) 18 times, sc in next 4 sc, ch 7, sk next 5 sc; join in first sc.

Rnd 3: Ch 1, sc in same sc as joining, *sc in each sc to next ch-7 sp, work 14 dc in next ch-7 sp; rep from * around; join in first sc.

Fasten off and weave in all tails.

Swirly Pigs

The three little piggies on this blanket are a reminder of a well-loved children's story.

Skill Level
■■□□ Easy

Size
Approx 36" diameter

Materials
Yarn: All yarns are light worsted-weight (3)
  MC: 500 yds (medium brown)
  CC: 500 yds (light brown)
  A: 80 yds (pink)
  B: 10 yds (black)
  C: 5 yds (white)
Hook: Size G-6 (4 mm) crochet hook
Notions: Tapestry needle

Gauge
5 rnds in sc = 2" diameter circle

Blanket
Unless otherwise instructed, work through back loops only when working in the round. Work through front loops only when working in rows.
With MC, ch 2.
Rnd 1: Sc 6 in 2nd ch from hook—6 sts.
Rnd 2: *With MC, sc 2; with CC, sc 2; rep from * twice—12 sts.
Rnd 3: *With MC, sc 2 in next st, sc in next st; with CC, sc 2 in next st, sc in next st; rep from * twice—18 sts.
Rnd 4: *With MC, sc 2 in next st, sc in next 2 sts; with CC, sc 2 in next st, sc in next 2 sts; rep from * twice—24 sts.
Rnd 5: *With MC, sc 2 in next st, sc in each of next 3 sts; with CC, sc 2 in next st, sc in each of next 3 sts; rep from * 3 times—30 sts.
Cont working rnds in this manner, inc 1 st on each of the 6 sides until each side has 76 sts—456 sts total.
Fasten off.

Pig Head (Make 3.)
With A, ch 2.
Rnd 1: Sc 6 in 2nd ch from hook—6 sts.
Rnd 2: Sc 2 in each st—12 sts.
Rnd 3: *Sc 2 in next st, sc in next st; rep from * 5 times—18 sts.
Rnd 4: *Sc 2 in next st, sc in next 2 sts; rep from * 5 times—24 sts.
Rnd 5: With B, *sc 2 in next st, sc in next 3 sts; rep from * 5 times—30 sts.
Rnd 6: With A, *sc 2 in next st, sc in next 4 sts; rep from * 5 times—36 sts.
Rnd 7: *Sc 2 in next st, sc in next 5 sts; rep from * 5 times—42 sts.
Rnd 8: *Sc 2 in next st, sc in next 6 sts; rep from * 5 times—48 sts.
Rnd 9: *Sc 2 in next st, sc in next 7 sts; rep from * 5 times—54 sts.
Rnd 10: *Sc 2 in next st, sc in next 8 sts; rep from * 5 times—60 sts.
Rnd 11: *Sc 2 in next st, sc in next 9 sts; rep from * 5 times—66 sts.
Fasten off with long tail.

Pig Ears (Make 6.)

With A, ch 3. Turn.

Row 1: Sc in 2nd ch from hook and in next ch. Turn—2 sts.

Rows 2-4: Ch 2, sc in 2nd ch from hook and in each st—6 sts at end of row 4.

To finish ears, sc 8 along each diagonal side.

Pig Nostrils (Make 6.)

With B, ch 2.

Sc 6 in 2nd ch from hook—6 sts.

Fasten off with long tail.

Pig Eyes (Make 6.)

Work through both loops.

With B, ch 2.

Rnd 1: Sc 6 in 2nd ch from hook—6 sts.

Rnd 2: With C, sc 2 in each st—12 sts.

Fasten off with long tail.

Assembly

Attach nostrils, ears, and eyes to pig head with whipstitch.

Joining to background

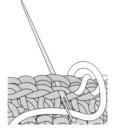

Joining pieces
along an edge

Joining medallions

Thread tapestry needle with yarn and tie knot at one end. Embroider mouth below nose as shown below. Bury end knot between pig face and blanket layers.

Attach pig heads to blanket on medium brown swirls as shown below.

Weave in ends.

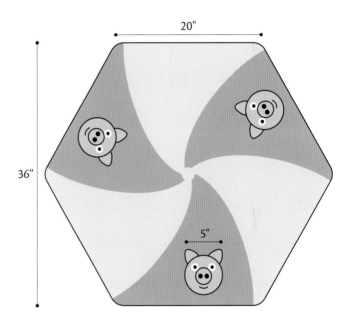

Chunky Sheep

Bulky-weight yarn and medallions mean that this blanket is quick to crochet and is great for crocheting on the go.

Skill Level
■■□□ Easy

Size
Approx 49" x 60"

Materials
Yarn:
- MC: 1020 yds of bulky-weight yarn (green) (5)
- A: 100 yds of bulky-weight yarn (white) (5)
- B: 50 yds of worsted-weight yarn (black) (4)

Hooks: Size K-10½ (6.5 mm) crochet hook, size H-8 (5 mm) crochet hook

Notions: Tapestry needle, jumbo tapestry needle (optional)

Gauge
6 rnds in sc = 4" diameter circle using K hook and bulky yarn

5 rnds in sc = 2" diameter circle using H hook and worsted yarn

Plain Medallions (Make 10.)
For this pattern, work through back loops only.

With MC and larger hook, ch 2.

Rnd 1: Sc 6 in 2nd ch from hook—6 sts.

Rnd 2: Sc 2 in each st—12 sts.

Rnd 3: *Sc 2 in next st, sc in next st; rep from * 5 times—18 sts.

Rnd 4: *Sc 2 in next st, sc in next 2 sts; rep from * 5 times—24 sts.

Rnd 5: *Sc 2 in next st, sc in next 3 sts; rep from * 5 times—30 sts.

Rnd 6: *Sc 2 in next st, sc in next 4 sts; rep from * 5 times—36 sts.

Rnd 7: *Sc 2 in next st, sc in next 5 sts; rep from * 5 times—42 sts.

Rnd 8: *Sc 2 in next st, sc in next 6 sts; rep from * 5 times—48 sts.

Rnd 9: *Sc 2 in next st, sc in next 7 sts; rep from * 5 times—54 sts.

Rnd 10: *Sc 2 in next st, sc in next 8 sts; rep from * 5 times—60 sts.

Rnd 11: *Sc 2 in next st, sc in next 9 sts; rep from * 5 times—66 sts.

Rnd 12: *Sc 2 in next st, sc in next 10 sts; rep from * 5 times—72 sts.

Rnd 13: *Sc 2 in next st, sc in next 11 sts; rep from * 5 times—78 sts.

Rnd 14: *Sc 2 in next st, sc in next 12 sts; rep from * 5 times—84 sts.

Rnd 15: *Sc 2 in next st, sc in next 13 sts; rep from * 5 times—90 sts.

Rnd 16: *Sc 2 in next st, sc in next 14 sts; rep from * 5 times—96 sts.

Rnd 17: *Sc 2 in next st, sc in next 15 sts; rep from * 5 times—102 sts.

Rnd 18: *Sc 2 in next st, sc in next 16 sts; rep from * 5 times—108 sts.

Rnd 19: *Sc 2 in next st, sc in next 17 sts; rep from * 5 times—114 sts.

Rnd 20: *Sc 2 in next st, sc in next 18 sts; rep from * 5 times—120 sts.

Fasten off with long tail (approx 24").

Sheep Medallions (Make 4.)

With A and larger hook, ch 2.

Rnd 1: Sc 6 in 2nd ch from hook—6 sts.

Rnd 2: Sc 2 in each st—12 sts.

Rnd 3: *Sc 2 in next st, sc in next st; rep from * 5 times—18 sts.

Rnd 4: *Sc 2 in next st, sc in next 2 sts; rep from * 5 times—24 sts.

Rnd 5: *Sc 2 in next st, sc in next 3 sts; rep from * 5 times—30 sts.

Rnd 6: *Sc 2 in next st, sc in next 4 sts; rep from * 5 times—36 sts.

Rnd 7: *Sc 2 in next st, sc in next 5 sts; rep from * 5 times—42 sts.

Rnd 8: *Sc 2 in next st, sc in next 6 sts; rep from * 5 times—48 sts.

Rnd 9: *Sc 2 in next st, sc in next 7 sts; rep from * 5 times—54 sts.

Rnd 10: *Sc 2 in next st, sc in next 8 sts; rep from * 5 times—60 sts.

Rnd 11: With MC, *sc 2 in next st, sc in next 9 sts; rep from * 5 times—66 sts.

Rnds 12–20: Follow instructions for rnds 12–20 for plain medallions.

Fasten off with long tail (approx 24").

Sheep Head (Make 4.)

With B and smaller hook, ch 2.

Rnd 1: Sc 6 in 2nd ch from hook—6 sts.

Rnd 2: Sc 2 in each st—12 sts.

Rnd 3: Sc in each st.

Rnd 4: *Sc 2 in next st, sc in next st; rep from * 5 times—18 sts.

Rnd 5: Sc in each st.

Rnd 6: *Sc 2 in next st, sc in next 2 sts; rep from * 5 times—24 sts.

Rnds 7–11: Sc in each st.

Rnd 12: *Sc2tog, sc in next 2 sts; rep from * 5 times—18 sts.

Rnd 13: *Sc2tog, sc in next st; rep from * 5 times—12 sts.

Fasten off with long tail.

Sheep Ears (Make 8.)

With B and smaller hook, ch 7. Turn.

Dc in 4th ch from hook and in next 4 chs (ch 3 counts as 1 dc—5 dc total).

Fasten off with long tail.

Finishing

Sheep Head

With long tail from head and tapestry needle, whip-stitch top of head closed.

With A, make 8 pupils by tying a square knot in a 4" length of yarn for each. Pull tails of knotted yard through sheep head for eyes and tie a knot on back to secure. Attach 2 pupils to each head.

Attach 2 ears to each head.

Using long tail of head, attach sheep head to center of sheep medallion as shown.

Assembling Medallions

Arrange medallions as shown and whipstitch tog using long tail, as shown on page 9.

Weave in ends.

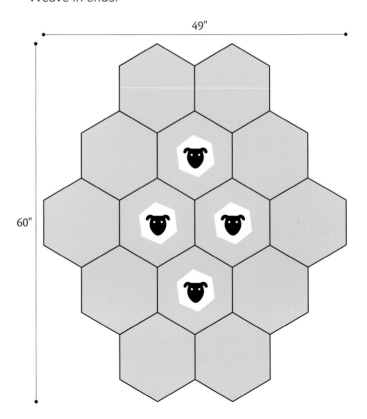

Scenic Koala

This scenic blanket features an adorable koala munching on a eucalyptus leaf. It works up quickly thanks to double crochet.

Skill Level
■■■□ Intermediate

Size
Approx 31" x 54"

Materials
Yarns: All yarns are light worsted-weight ③
- MC: 960 yds (blue)
- CC: 300 yds (brown)
- A: 100 yds (gray)
- B: 50 yds (green)
- C: 5 yds (black)
- D: 5 yds (white)

Hook: Size H-8 (5 mm) crochet hook

Notions: Tapestry needle

Gauge
15 sts and 8 rows = 4" x 4" in dc

Blanket
Unless otherwise instructed, work through back loops only when working in the round. Work through front loops only when working in rows.

Ch 3 counts as 1 dc at beg of every row.

With MC, ch 202.

Row 1: Dc in 4th ch from hook and in each ch. Turn (3 ch counts as 1 dc—200 dc total).

Rows 2-7: Ch 3, dc in each st. Turn.

Rows 8-17: With CC, ch 3, dc in each st. Turn.

Row 18: With MC, ch 3, dc in next 74 sts; with CC, dc in next 15 sts; with MC, dc in rem 110 sts. Turn.

Row 19: Ch 3, dc in next 110 sts; with CC, dc in next 15 sts; with MC, dc in rem 74 sts.

Row 20: Ch 3, dc in next 72 sts; with CC, dc in next 15 sts; with MC, dc in rem 112 sts. Turn.

Row 21: Ch 3, dc in next 112 sts; with CC, dc in next 15 sts; with MC, dc in rem 72 sts. Turn.

Row 22: Ch 3, dc in next 70 sts; with CC, dc in next 15 sts; with MC, dc in rem 114 sts. Turn.

Row 23: Ch 3, dc in next 114 sts; with CC, dc in next 15 sts; with MC, dc in rem 70 sts.

Cont in this manner, working 2 less sts in MC at beg of every even-numbered row; this will move the 15 CC sts closer to top of blanket by 2 sts to create a 45°-angle branch; there will then be 2 more sts in MC at end of row. Cont until you have worked 61 rows. Fasten off.

Leaves (Make 10.)
With B, ch 19. Turn.

Sl st in 2nd ch from hook and in next ch, sc in next ch, hdc in next 2 chs, dc in next 2 chs, tr in next 4 chs, dc in next 2 chs, hdc in next 2 chs, sc in next ch, sl st in next 2 chs. Rotate piece clockwise and with RS still facing you, work into bottom loops of foundation ch; rep from * to * once.

Fasten off with long tail.

Koala Head/Body (Make 1 body and 1 head.)
With A, ch 2.

Rnd 1: Sc 6 in 2nd ch from hook—6 sts.

Rnd 2: Sc 2 in each st—12 sts.

Rnd 3: *Sc 2 in next st, sc in next st; rep from * 5 times—18 sts.

Rnd 4: *Sc 2 in next st, sc in next 2 sts; rep from * 5 times—24 sts.

Rnd 5: *Sc 2 in next st, sc in next 3 sts; rep from * 5 times—30 sts.

Rnd 6: *Sc 2 in next st, sc in next 4 sts; rep from * 5 times—36 sts.

Rnd 7: *Sc 2 in next st, sc in next 5 sts; rep from * 5 times—42 sts.

Rnd 8: *Sc 2 in next st, sc in next 6 sts; rep from * 5 times—48 sts.

Rnd 9: *Sc 2 in next st, sc in next 7 sts; rep from * 5 times—54 sts.

Rnd 10: *Sc 2 in next st, sc in next 8 sts; rep from * 5 times—60 sts.

Rnd 11: *Sc 2 in next st, sc in next 9 sts; rep from * 5 times—66 sts.

Rnd 12: *Sc 2 in next st, sc in next 10 sts; rep from * 5 times—72 sts.

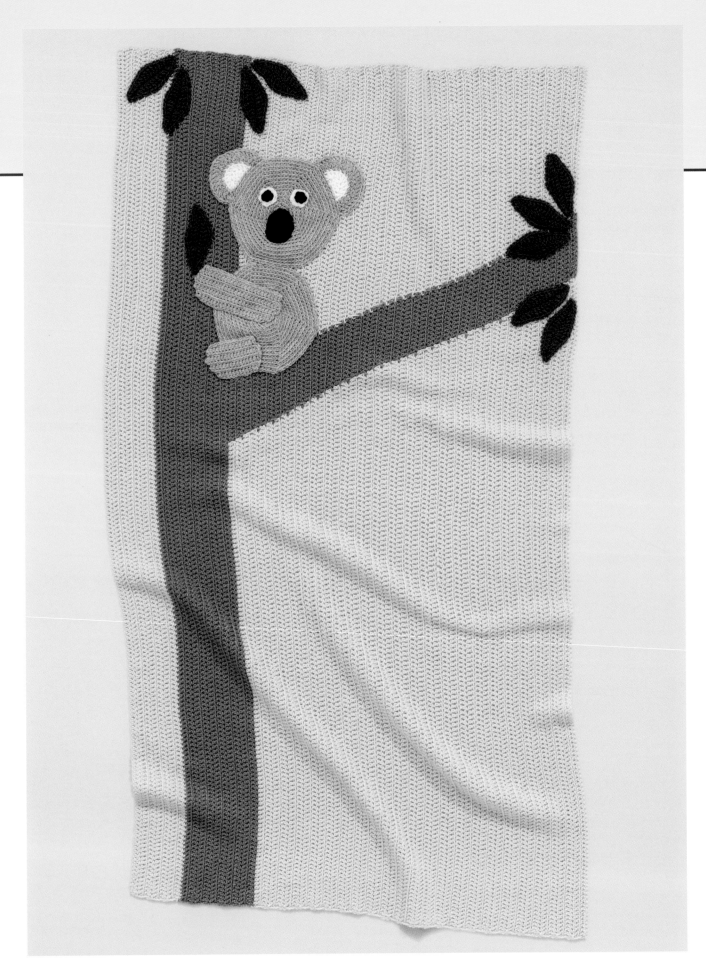

Rnd 13: *Sc 2 in next st, sc in next 11 sts; rep from * 5 times—78 sts.

Rnd 14: *Sc 2 in next st, sc in next 12 sts; rep from * 5 times—84 sts.

Rnd 15: *Sc 2 in next st, sc in next 13 sts; rep from * 5 times—90 sts.

Fasten off with long tail.

Koala Arm

With A, ch 23. Turn.

Row 1: Sc in 2nd ch from hook and in each st. Turn—22 sts.

Rows 2–5: Ch 2, sc in 2nd ch from hook and in each st. Turn—26 sts at end of row 5.

Rows 6–8: Ch 1, sc to last st, leaving last st unworked. Turn—23 sts at end of row 8.

Fasten off with long tail.

Koala Leg

With A, ch 13. Turn.

Row 1: Sc in 2nd ch from hook and in each ch. Turn—12 sts.

Rows 2–5: Ch 2, sc in 2nd ch from hook and in each st. Turn—16 sts at end of row 5.

Rows 6–8: Ch 1, sc to last st, leaving last st unworked—13 sts at end of row 8.

Fasten off with long tail.

Koala Ears (Make 2.)

With D, ch 4.

Row 1: Dc 5 times in 4th ch from hook. Turn (ch 3 counts as 1 dc—6 dc total).

Row 2: Ch 3 (counts as 1 dc), dc in st at base of ch 3, dc 2 in each rem st. Turn—12 sts.

Row 3: With A, ch 3 (counts as 1 dc), dc in st at base of ch 3, dc in next st, *dc 2 in next st, dc 1 in next st; rep from * 4 times. Turn—18 sts.

Row 4: Ch 3 (counts as 1 dc), dc in st at base of ch 3, dc in next 2 sts, *dc 2 in next st, dc 1 in each of next 2 sts; rep from * 4 times—24 sts.

Fasten off with long tail.

Koala Nose

With C, ch 2.

Rnd 1: Sc 6 in 2nd ch from hook—6 sts.

Rnd 2: Sc 2 in each st—12 sts.

Rnd 3: *Sc 2 in next st, sc in next st; rep from * 5 times—18 sts.

Rnd 4: [*Hdc 2 in next st, hdc in each of next 2 sts; rep from * once, sl st in each of next 3 sts]; rep instructions in brackets once—22 sts.

Fasten off with long tail.

Koala Eyes (Make 2.)

Work through both loops.

With C, ch 2.

Rnd 1: Sc 6 in 2nd ch from hook—6 sts.

Rnd 2: With D, sc 2 in each st—12 sts.

Fasten off with long tail.

Assembly

Use whipstitch to join pieces.

Attach nose, ears, and eyes to koala head. Attach koala head and body to blanket body. Attach arm and leg to koala body. Attach leaves to blanket. Weave in ends.

Keeping Koala Flat

After you attach the koala head and body, you may find that the middle of the head and body stick out a bit from the blanket. To remedy this, also attach the head and body to the blanket at round 7.

Rainbow

The lining on this colorful, quick-to-crochet blanket adds warmth and softness and makes the blanket reversible.

Skill Level
■■□□ Easy

Size
28" x 36"

Materials
Yarn: 60% cotton, 40% acrylic microfiber worsted-weight yarn (4)
300 yds *each* of cream, aqua, and lime
100 yds *each* of brown, rose, and orange
Hook: Size I-9 (5.5 mm) crochet hook
Notions: Tapestry needle, 1¼ yds of cotton fabric at least 36" wide for lining (optional; be sure to pre-shrink), sewing needle and sewing thread

Gauge
13 sts and 11 rows = 4" in counterpane st

Counterpane Stitch
All rows: Ch 2 (do not count as st), YO, insert hook in first st, YO, draw yarn through this st and first lp on hook, YO, draw yarn through rem lps, *YO, insert hook in next st, YO, draw yarn through this st and first lp on hook, YO, draw yarn through rem lps; rep from * across.

Blanket
First block: Referring to chart above right, select color and ch 19. Set-up row (counts as row 1): YO, insert hook in 3rd ch from hook (do not count as st), YO, draw yarn through ch and first lp on hook, YO, draw yarn through rem lps, *YO, insert hook in next ch, YO, draw yarn through ch and first lp on hook, YO, draw through rem lps; rep from * across row—17 sts, turn. Work counterpane st for 13 more rows—1 color block complete.
Next 6 blocks: Change color and work 14 rows in counterpane st. Cont working blocks of color as

indicated in chart until you have 7 blocks of color in a vertical strip. Make 6 vertical strips.

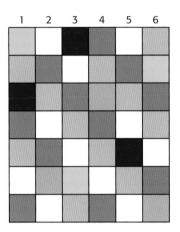

Each strip is worked vertically
in counterpane st—6 strips total.
Each square is 17 sts wide by 14 rows tall.

Finishing
Sew strips tog using overcast seam as follows: *Thread project yarn through tapestry needle, lay pieces to be joined RS up and side by side, insert needle into BL of edge stitch from each piece, put the yarn through (not too tightly); rep from * to end of seam.
Edging: With RS facing you, work edges as follows: Using different yarn color for each edge of the blanket, work 1 row counterpane st along right selvage, working 1 edge st for every row. Change color and work 1 row counterpane st along upper edge, working 1 edge st for every st. Change color and work 1 row counterpane st along left selvage, working 1 edge st for every row. Change color and work 1 row counterpane st along lower edge, working 1 edge st for every ch. Join last E st to first D st with a sl st.
Weave in ends. Block blanket according to instructions on yarn label.
Lining: Preshrink cotton fabric, cut fabric to 28" x 36", serge edges or fold under ½" all the way around, pin fabric to WS of blanket and hand stitch in place with sewing needle and thread.

Baby Stripes

Crochet this delightful baby-shower gift in a couple of days with oh-so-soft bulky-weight yarn.

Skill Level
■■■□ Intermediate

Size
32" x 45"

Materials
Yarn: All yarns are 100% nylon bulky-weight yarn (5)
  A: 820 yds (white)
  B: 245 yds (lavender)
  C: 245 yds (blue)
  D: 245 yds (pink)
  E: 245 yds (green)
Hook: Size H-8 (5 mm) crochet hook or size to obtain gauge
Notions: Tapestry needle

Gauge
14 dc and 7 rows = 4"

Pattern Stitch
Cluster (CL): Ch 3, (keeping last lp of each tr on hook, work 2 tr in same st or ch). YO and draw through all 3 lps on hook. CLs will lie sideways as you work patt.

Blanket
Blanket is worked from side to side, beg near center. To change colors, work until last 2 lps of st rem on hook, draw new color through; cut old color.

First Side
With A, ch 156.
Row 1 (WS): Dc in 4th ch from hook (beg 3 sk chs count as first dc) and in each rem ch. Turn—154 dc.
Row 2 (RS): Ch 1, sc in first 2 dc, *CL, sk next 2 dc, sc in next 2 dc; rep from * to last 4 sts, CL, sk next 2 dc, sc in next dc and in top of beg 3 sk chs. Turn—38 CLs.

Row 3: Ch 2 (counts as a dc on this and following rows), dc in next sc, ch 2, sk next CL, *dc in next 2 dc, ch 2, sk next CL; rep from * across, dc in last 2 sc. Turn—38 ch-2 sps.
Row 4: Ch 2, dc in next dc, work 2 dc in next ch-2 sp, *dc in next 2 sc, work 2 dc in next ch-2 sp; rep from * across, dc in last dc and in top of beg ch 2, changing to B in last dc. Turn—154 dc.
Row 5: With B, ch 2, dc in each dc and in top of beg ch 2, changing to A in last dc. Turn.
Row 6: With A, rep row 2, changing to B in last sc. Turn.
Rows 7 and 8: With B, rep rows 3 and 4, changing to C in last dc of row 8. Turn.
Row 9: With C, rep row 5, changing to B in last dc. Turn.
Row 10: With B, rep row 2, changing to C in last sc. Turn.
Rows 11 and 12: With C, rep rows 3 and 4, changing to D in last dc of row 12. Turn.
Row 13: With D, rep row 5, changing to C in last dc. Turn.
Row 14: With C, rep row 2, changing to D in last sc. Turn.
Rows 15 and 16: With D, rep rows 3 and 4, changing to E in last dc of row 16. Turn.
Row 17: With E, rep row 5, changing to D in last dc. Turn.
Row 18: With D, rep row 2, changing to E in last sc. Turn.
Rows 19 and 20: With E, rep rows 3 and 4, changing to A in last dc of row 20. Turn.
Row 21: With A, rep row 5, changing to E in last dc. Turn.
Row 22: With E, rep row 2. At end of row, fasten off and weave in tails.

Second Side

Hold first side with RS facing you and beg ch at top; join A in first unused lp of beg ch.

Row 1 (RS): Ch 2 (counts as a dc on this and following rows), dc in each rem unused lp. Turn—154 dc.

Row 2: Ch 2, dc in next dc, ch 1, sk next dc, *dc in next dc, ch 1, sk next dc; rep from * to last st, dc in top of beg ch 2. Turn—76 ch-1 sps.

Row 3: Ch 2, dc in each ch-1 sp, in each dc, and in top of beg ch 2. Turn—154 dc.

Rows 4 and 5: Rep rows 2 and 3.

Rows 6 and 7: Ch 2, dc in each dc and in top of beg ch 2. Turn.

Rows 8–13: Rep rows 2–7.

Rows 14–18: Rep rows 2–6.

Rows 19–39: Beg with A and changing colors as for first side, rep rows 2–22 of first side.

Fasten off and weave in tails.

Ties (optional)

With B, make 2 chains, 60" long. Weave in tails. With E, make 4 more ties. Weave 1 B tie through ch-1 sps on each side of center row; weave 1 E tie through each of rem 4 rows with ch-1 sps. Referring to photo below, tie bows at each end.

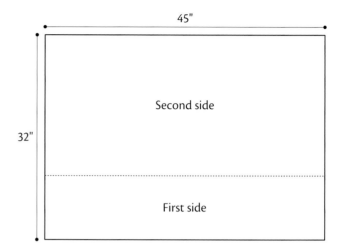

Baby Bobbles

Tiny navy and green bobbles chase each other across this brightly striped blanket.

Skill Level
◼◼◼◻ Intermediate

Size
32" x 36"

Materials
Yarn: All yarns are 55% nylon, 45% acrylic DK-weight ③
- **A:** 950 yds (white)
- **B:** 570 yds (navy)
- **C:** 570 yds (green)

Hook: Size G-6 (4 mm) crochet hook or size to obtain gauge

Notions: Tapestry needle

Gauge
20 dc and 12 rows = 4"

Pattern Stitches
Bobble: Keeping last lp of each dc on hook, 5 dc in next st, YO, draw through all 6 lps on hook, ch 1, push bobble to RS.

Front-post cluster (FPCL): Keeping last lp of each dc on hook, 2 dc around post of next dc on row below, YO, and draw through all 3 lps on hook. On working row, sk st behind FPCL.

Blanket
To change color, work until 2 lps of last st rem on hook. With new color, YO and draw through 2 lps on hook. Cut old color.

Beg at lower edge with A, ch 153.

Foundation row: Sc in 2nd ch from hook and in each rem ch. Turn—152 sc.

Row 1 (RS): Cont with A, ch 2 (counts as first dc on this and following rows), dc in each sc, changing to B in last dc. Turn.

Row 2: With B, ch 1, sc in first dc and in next 7 dc, bobble in next dc, (sc in next 9 dc, bobble in next dc) 14 times, sc in next 2 dc and in top of beg ch 2, changing to A in last dc. Turn.

Row 3: With A, ch 2, dc in each sc and in ch 1 of each bobble, changing to C in last dc. Turn.

Row 4: With C, ch 1, sc in first 3 dc, bobble in next dc, (sc in next 9 dc, bobble in next dc) 14 times, sc in next 7 dc and in top of beg ch 2, changing to A in last dc. Turn.

Row 5: With A, ch 2, dc in each sc and in ch-1 sp of each bobble. Turn.

Row 6: Cont with A, ch 2, dc in each dc and in top of beg ch 2. Turn.

Row 7: Cont with A, ch 2, dc in next 2 dc, FPCL around post of next dc on row below, (dc in next 9 dc, FPCL around post of next dc on row below) 14 times, dc in next 7 dc and in top of beg ch 2, changing to B in last dc. Turn.

Row 8: With B, ch 2, dc in each dc, in each FPCL, and in top of beg ch 2, changing to C in last dc. Turn.

Row 9: With C, ch 2, dc in next 7 dc, FPCL around post of next dc on row below, (dc in next 9 dc, FPCL around post of next dc on row below) 14 times, dc in next 2 dc and in top of beg ch 2, changing to B in last dc. Turn.

Row 10: With B, ch 2, dc in each dc, in each FPCL, and in top of beg ch 2, changing to A in last dc. Turn.

Row 11: With A, ch 2, dc in next 2 dc, FPCL around post of next dc on row below, (dc in next 9 dc, FPCL around post of next dc on row below) 14 times, dc in next 7 dc and in top of beg ch 2. Turn.

Row 12: Cont with A, dc in each dc, in each FPCL, and in top of beg ch 2. Turn.

Row 13: Cont with A, ch 2, dc in next 7 dc, FPCL around post of next dc on row below, (dc in next 9 dc, work FPCL around post of next dc on row below) 14 times, dc in next 2 dc and in top of beg ch 2, changing to C in last dc. Turn.

Row 14: With C, ch 1, sc in first dc and in next 7 sc, bobble in next dc, (sc in next 9 dc, bobble in next dc) 14 times, sc in next 2 dc and in top of beg ch 2, changing to A in last dc. Turn.

Row 15: With A, ch 2, dc in each sc and in ch 1 of each bobble, changing to B in last dc. Turn.

Row 16: With B, ch 1, sc in first 3 dc, bobble in next dc, (sc in next 9 dc, bobble in next dc) 14 times, sc in next 7 dc and in top of beg ch 2, changing to A in last dc. Turn.

Row 17: With A, ch 2, dc in each sc and in ch 1 of each bobble. Turn.

Row 18: Cont with A, ch 2, dc in each dc and in top of beg ch 2. Turn.

Row 19: Cont with A, ch 2, dc in next 2 dc, FPCL around post of next dc on row below, (dc in next 9 dc, FPCL around post of next dc on row below) 14 times, dc in next 7 dc and in top of beg ch 2, changing to C in last dc. Turn.

Row 20: With C, ch 2, dc in each dc, in each FPCL, and in top of beg ch 2, changing to B in last dc. Turn.

Row 21: With B, ch 2, dc in next 7 dc, FPCL around post of next dc on row below, (dc in next 9 dc, FPCL around post of next dc on row below) 14 times, dc in next 2 dc and in top of beg ch 2, changing to C in last dc. Turn.

Row 22: With C, ch 2, dc in each dc, in each FPCL, and in top of beg ch 2, changing to A in last dc. Turn.

Row 23: With A, ch 2, dc in next 2 dc, FPCL around post of next dc on row below, (dc in next 9 dc, FPCL around post of next dc on row below) 14 times, dc in next 7 dc and in top of beg ch 2. Turn.

Row 24: Cont with A, ch 2, dc in each dc, in each FPCL, and in top of beg ch 2. Turn.

Row 25: Cont with A, ch 2, dc in next 7 dc, FPCL around post of next dc on row below, (dc in next 9 dc, FPCL around post of next dc on row below) 14 times, dc in 2 dc and in top of beg ch 2, changing to B in last dc. Turn.

Rows 26–121: Work rows 2–25.

Rows 122–137: Rep rows 2–17. At end of row 137, do not turn.

Edging

Cont with A along side edge, ch 1, *sc in edge of each sc row and 2 sc in edge of each dc row*; working along lower edge in unused lps of beg ch, 3 sc in first lp, sc in next 150 lps, 3 sc in next lp; working along next side; rep from * to * once; working along top edge, 3 sc in top of beg ch 2, sc in next 150 dc, 3 sc in next dc; join in first sc. Fasten off.

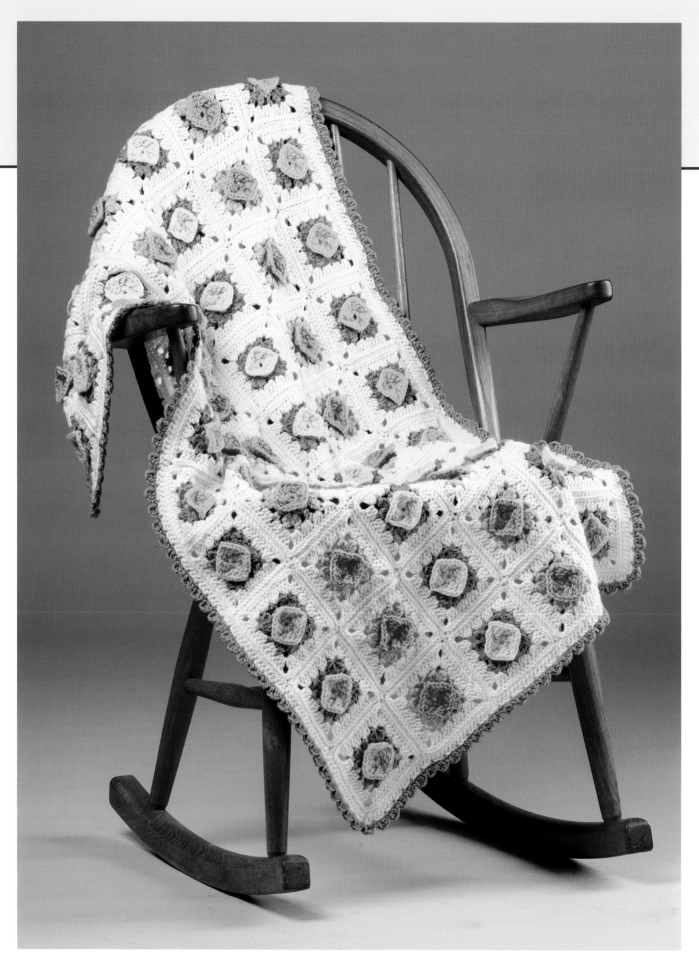

Rosebuds for My Baby

Pretty rows of rosebuds line up side by side on this delightful, updated granny-square blanket.

Skill Level
■■■□ Intermediate

Size
30" x 42"

Materials
Yarn: All yarns are 100% superwash worsted-weight wool (**4**)

MC: 660 yds (off-white)
A: 220 yds (pink)
B: 220 yds (orange)
C: 220 yds (yellow)
D: 220 yds (green)
E: 440 yds (dark green)

Hook: Size G-6 (4 mm) crochet hook or size to obtain gauge

Notions: Tapestry needle

Gauge
One motif = 4" x 4"

Pattern Stitch
Cluster (CL): Keeping last lp of each dc on hook, work 3 dc in same dc, YO and draw through all 4 lps on hook.

Motif A (Make 30.)
Rnd 1: With A, ch 4, work 15 dc in 4th ch from hook (3 sk chs count as a dc); join in top of beg ch 4—16 dc.

Rnd 2: Ch 2, work 3 FPdc around post of beg ch on rnd 1, ch 1, sk next dc, FPdc around post of next dc, ch 1, sk next dc, *work 3 FPdc around post of next dc, ch 1, sk next dc, work FPdc around post of next dc, ch 1, sk next dc; rep from * 2 times, sk beg ch 2; join in first FPdc— four 3-FPdc groups. Fasten off A and weave in tails.

Rnd 3: Working behind rnd 2, join D in first sk dc on rnd 1, ch 1, sc in same dc, ch 3; for corner, (CL, ch 3, CL) in next sk dc, ch 3, *sc in next sk dc, ch 3; for corner, (CL, ch 3, CL) in next sk dc, ch 3; rep from * around; join in first sc—four 2-CL corners. Fasten off D.

Rnd 4: Join MC in any corner ch-3 sp, ch 3 (counts as a dc on this and following rnds), work 2 dc in same sp, 3 dc in each of next 2 ch-3 sps, *work (3 dc, ch 3, 3 dc) in next corner ch-3 sp, 3 dc in each of next 2 ch-3 sps; rep from * 2 times, work 3 dc in same corner ch-3 sp as beg ch, ch 3; join in top of beg ch 3—12 dc on each side.

Rnd 5: Ch 1, sc in same ch and in next 11 dc, work 5 sc in next corner ch-3 sp, *sc in next 12 dc, work 5 sc in next corner ch-3 sp; rep from * 2 times; join in first sc. Fasten off, leaving an 18" tail for sewing. Fasten off.

Motif B (Make 20.)
Make same as motif A using color B on rnds 1 and 2, color E on rnd 3, and MC on rnds 4 and 5.

Motif C (Make 20.)
Make same as motif A using color C on rnds 1 and 2, color E on rnd 3, and MC on rnds 4 and 5.

Finishing
With RS tog and using tapestry needle and long tails, sew A motifs tog to form 3 rows of 10 motifs. Sew B motifs tog to form 2 rows of 10 motifs. Sew C motifs tog to form 2 rows of 10 motifs. Referring to diagram, sew motif rows tog with MC to form blanket.

Edging

Hold blanket with RS facing you; join MC in BL of any corner sc.

Rnd 1: Ch 3, dc in same lp, dc in BL of each sc and in each motif joining to next corner, *work 3 dc in BL of corner sc, dc in BL of each sc and in each motif joining to next corner; rep from * 2 times; join in top of beg ch 3—819 sc. Fasten off MC.

Rnd 2: Join color E in any corner dc, ch 1, sc in same dc; *ch 3, keeping last lp of each dc on hook, work 2 dc in first ch of ch 3 just made, YO and draw through all 3 lps on hook, sk next 2 dc, sc in next dc; rep from * around, ending last rep by joining in first sc. Fasten off E.

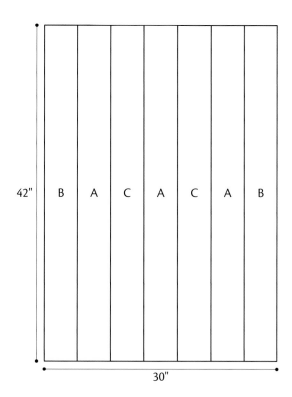

Striped Bear

Not only is this blanket adorable, it's also suited to children of any age—and sure to be treasured for years!

Skill Level
■■■▶ Experienced

Size
Approx 40" x 44"

Materials
Yarns: All yarns are light worsted-weight ③

    MC: 1150 yds (yellow)

    CC: 840 yds (green)

    A: 90 yds (medium brown)

    B: 25 yds (light brown)

    C: 5 yds (dark brown)

Hook: Size H-8 (5 mm) crochet hook or size to obtain gauge

Notions: 4 locking stitch markers, yarn bobbins (optional), tapestry needle

Gauge
18 sts and 15 rows = 4" x 4" in sc

Foundation Chains
For the strips of the blanket to fit together properly, it's important that your foundation chains aren't too tight. If you tend to crochet tightly, try making the chains with a hook one size larger than called for (in this case, size I), and then continue crocheting with your regular size hook.

Plain Strip (Make 3.)
Unless otherwise instructed, work through front loops.
With MC, ch 176. Turn.

Row 1: Sc in 2nd ch from hook and in each ch. Turn— 175 sts.

Row 2: Ch 1, sc in each st. Turn.

Rows 3–16: Ch 2, sc in 2nd ch from hook and in each st. Turn—189 sts after row 16.

Row 17: Ch 2, sc in 2nd ch from hook and in each st to last st. Turn, leaving last st unworked.

Rows 18–31: Ch 1, sc to last st. Turn, leaving last st unworked—175 sts after row 31.

Row 32: Rep row 2.

Fasten off. Weave in ends.

Using Bobbins with Color Changes
The teddy-bear strip has a lot of color changes, which can be a bit complicated. There are two ways to handle multiple color changes. One, you can cut the yarn every time you switch colors. This option leaves you with lots of ends to weave in at the end. The second option is to leave the yarn uncut and continue using the yarn on the next row. But having so many strands of yarn hanging off your work can leave you with a tangled mess. A solution to this problem is to use yarn bobbins.

    Yarn bobbins are cardboard or plastic devices meant to hold small amounts of yarn. You simply wind a small amount of yarn on the bobbin, which keep the ends from getting tangled. If you keep your yarn tidy, then you can say goodbye to a frustrating color-change experience!

Teddy-Bear Strip (Make 2.)
Unless otherwise instructed, work through front loops.
With CC, ch 176. Turn.

Row 1: Sc in 2nd ch from hook and in each ch. Turn— 175 sts.

Row 2: Ch 1, sc in each st. Turn.

Beg working from Teddy-Bear Charts (page 29) on next row.

Row 3: Ch 2, sc in 2nd ch from hook and in next 3 sts, pm in last st to indicate st before beg of chart. Work row 1 of right-end chart over next 27 sts, sc in next st and pm to indicate st after chart ends, sc in next 113 sts, pm in last st to indicate st before beg of second chart, work row 1 of left-end chart over next 27 sts, sc in next st and pm to indicate st after chart ends, sc in next 3 sts—176 sts.

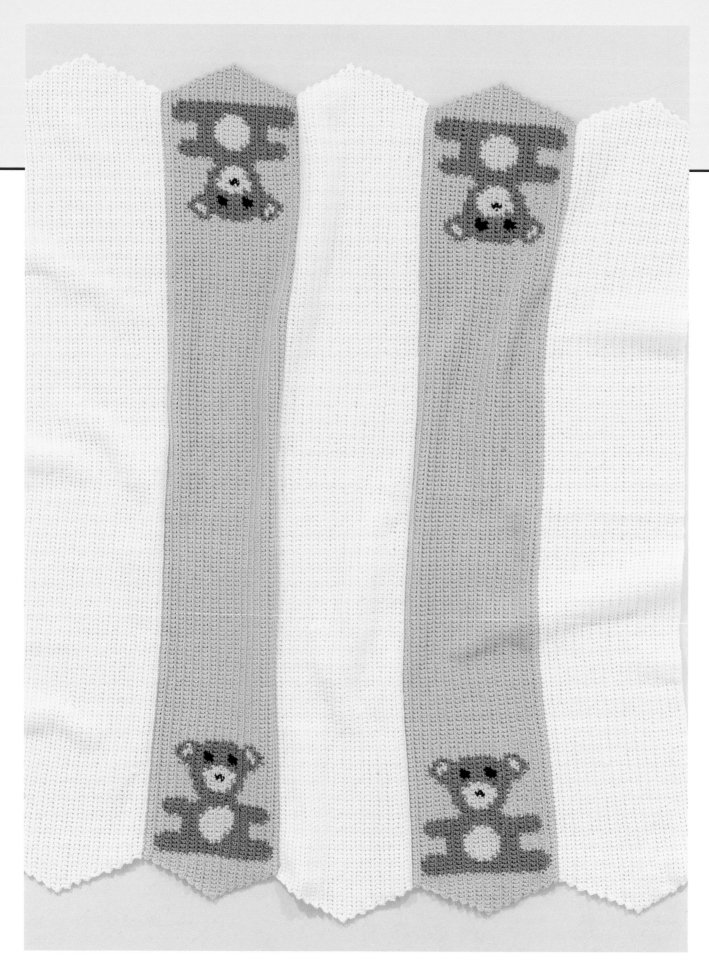

Cont working chart between markers at each end of strip as follows:

Rows 4-16: Ch 2, sc in 2nd ch from hook and in each st. Turn—189 sts after row 16.

Row 17: Ch 2, sc in 2nd ch from hook and in each st to last st. Turn, leaving last st unworked—189 sts.

Rows 18-30: Ch 1, sc to last st. Turn, leaving last st unworked—176 sts after row 30.

Chart ends on row 30.

Row 31: Ch 1, sc to last st. Turn, leaving last st unworked—175 sts.

Row 32: Ch 1, sc in each st.

Fasten off.

Keeping Track of Your Chart

The pattern instructs you to place stitch markers to keep track of where the chart begins and ends. This is really important for this pattern, because the edges contain increases, meaning that you can't always work the chart a certain number of stitches from the edge.

Finishing

Arrange strips as shown and join them using sl-st crochet.

Weave in ends.

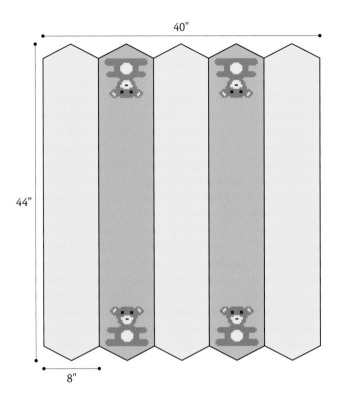

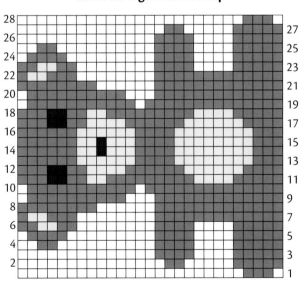

Chart for left end of strip

Chart for right end of strip

Key

■	A
□	B
■	C
□	CC

Read odd-numbered rows from right to left.
Read even-numbered rows from left to right.

Hoodie Bird

Worsted-weight yarn and single crochet make this blanket thick and cozy. Children will love the hood for games of peekaboo!

Skill Level
■□□□ Beginner

Size
Approx 31" x 31"

Materials
Yarns: All yarns are worsted-weight (4)
  MC: 1050 yds (blue)
  A: 60 yds (orange)
  B: 5 yds, white
  C: 5 yds, black
Hook: Size H-8 (5 mm) crochet hook or size to obtain gauge
Notions: Tapestry needle

Gauge
9 rnds in sc = 4" x 4"

Blanket
Unless otherwise instructed, work through back loops only when working in the round. Work through front loops only when working in rows.
With MC, ch 2.
Rnd 1: Sc 8 in 2nd ch from hook—8 sts.
Rnd 2: *Sc 3 in next st, sc in next st; rep from * 3 times—16 sts.
Rnd 3: Sc in next st, *sc 3 in next st, sc in next 3 sts; rep from * 2 times, sc 3 in next st, sc in next 2 sts—24 sts.
Rnd 4: Sc in next 2 sts, *sc 3 in next st, sc in next 5 sts; rep from * 2 times, sc 3 in next st, sc in next 3 sts—32 sts.
Rnd 5: Sc in next 3 sts, *sc 3 in next st, sc in next 7 sts; rep from * 2 times, sc 3 in next st, sc in next 4 sts—40 sts.
Cont working rnds in patt as established, working 3 sc in center st of each corner and 2 more sc on each side of square until blanket measures approx 30" square.
Fasten off.

Counting Rounds in the Blanket
Are you tired of counting? After a couple of rounds, you'll notice that there is a hole in each of the four corners of the blanket, which is created every time you single crochet three times in the same stitch. All you need to remember to keep your square pattern is to single crochet three times into the center stitch when you see this hole. The rest of the time, you just single crochet around and around!

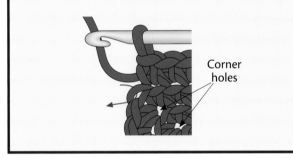

Corner holes

Birdie Hood
The hood is a triangle that will fit neatly into the corner of your blanket. The shape is created by increasing two stitches at the beg of each row.
With MC, ch 3. Turn.
Row 1: Sc in 2nd ch from hook and in next st. Turn—2 sts.
Row 2: Ch 3, sc in 2nd ch from hook and in next ch, sc in each st across. Turn—4 sts.
Rows 3-33: Ch 3, sc in 2nd ch from hook and in next ch, sc in each st across. Turn—66 sts after rnd 33.
To finish hood, sc 49 along each side of diagonal (this averages 3 sts for every 2 rows).
Fasten off with long tail.

Feet

Big Foot Circle (Make 2.)
With A, ch 2.
Rnd 1: Sc 6 in 2nd ch from hook—6 sts.
Rnd 2: Sc 2 in each st—12 sts.
Rnd 3: *Sc 2 in next st, sc in next st; rep from * 5 times—18 sts.
Rnd 4: *Sc 2 in next st, sc in next 2 sts; rep from * 5 times—24 sts.
Rnd 5: *Sc 2 in next st, sc in next 3 sts; rep from * 5 times—30 sts.
Rnd 6: *Sc 2 in next st, sc in next 4 sts; rep from * 5 times—36 sts.
Rnd 7: *Sc 2 in next st, sc in next 5 sts; rep from * 5 times—42 sts.
Rnd 8: *Sc 2 in next st, sc in next 6 sts; rep from * 5 times—48 sts.
Rnd 9: *Sc 2 in next st, sc in next 7 sts; rep from * 5 times—54 sts.
Rnd 10: *Sc 2 in next st, sc in next 8 sts; rep from * 5 times—60 sts.
Fasten off with long tail.

Toes (Make 6.)
With A, ch 4. Turn.
Row 1: Dc 5 in 4th ch from hook. Turn—ch 3 counts as 1 dc, 6 dc total.
Row 2: Ch 3 (counts as 1 dc), dc in st at base of ch 3, dc 2 in next 5 sts—12 sts.
Fasten off with long tail.

Assemble feet: Attach flat sides of 3 toes to each foot circle as shown.

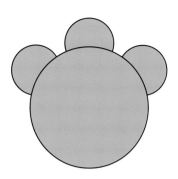

Beak

With A, ch 3. Turn.
Row 1: Sc in 2nd ch from hook and in next st. Turn—2 sts.
Rows 2-10: Ch 2, sc in 2nd ch from hook, sc in each st—11 sts after row 10.
To finish beak, sc 9 along each diagonal side.
Fasten off with long tail.

Eyes (Make 2.)

Work through both loops.
With C, ch 2.
Rnd 1: Sc 6 in 2nd ch from hook—6 sts.
Rnd 2: With B, sc 2 in each st—12 sts.
Fasten off with long tail.

Assembly

Whipstitch eyes and beak to hood.
Place WS of hood on RS of one corner of blanket with edges aligned. With RS facing you, and working through both hood and blanket, sc hood to blanket.
Cont sc along rem sides of blanket until you reach beg of where hood is attached.
Whipstitch feet to blanket.
Weave in ends.